Celebrated Lyrical Sol

9 Solos in Romantic Styles for Early Intermediate to Intermediate Pianists

Robert D. Vandall

Gina Chaleunphonh

Students all love to play fast and showy pieces, but there is another side to performing that needs to be developed: the lyrical side. Beautiful melodies need to be shaped musically and balanced properly against the accompaniment. The ability to bend the tempo and play with flexibility also results in expressive playing. Colorful harmonies and their movement can create a sound world that can be molded into beautiful moments as well.

The pieces in *Celebrated Lyrical Solos, Book 3* are designed to aid students with musicality when playing lyrical music. I have endeavored to include pieces with a variety of tempos and moods. While every piece may not necessarily focus on lyrical styles throughout, each has a section that will help students develop skills in lyrical playing. Look for the many ways that the pieces in these books can be balanced and molded into something beautiful. Feel, listen and enjoy the many lyrical moods of these solos.

Robert D. Vandall

Contents

Copyright © MMVIII by Alfred Publishing Co., Inc.
All rights reserved.   Printed in USA.
ISBN-10: 0-7390-5076-1
ISBN-13: 978-0-7390-5076-7

Evening Shadows

Robert D. Vandall

4

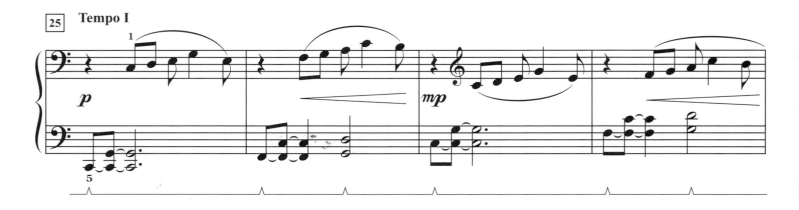

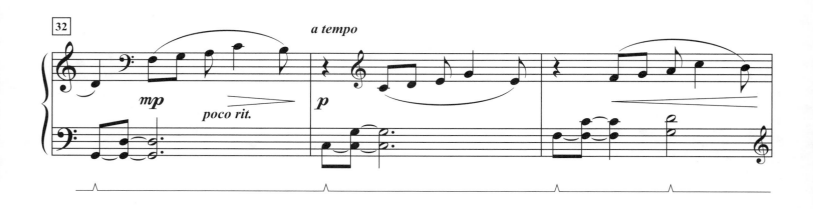

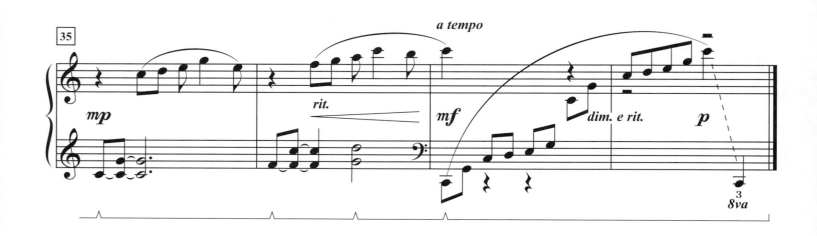

Atwood Lake

Robert D. Vandall

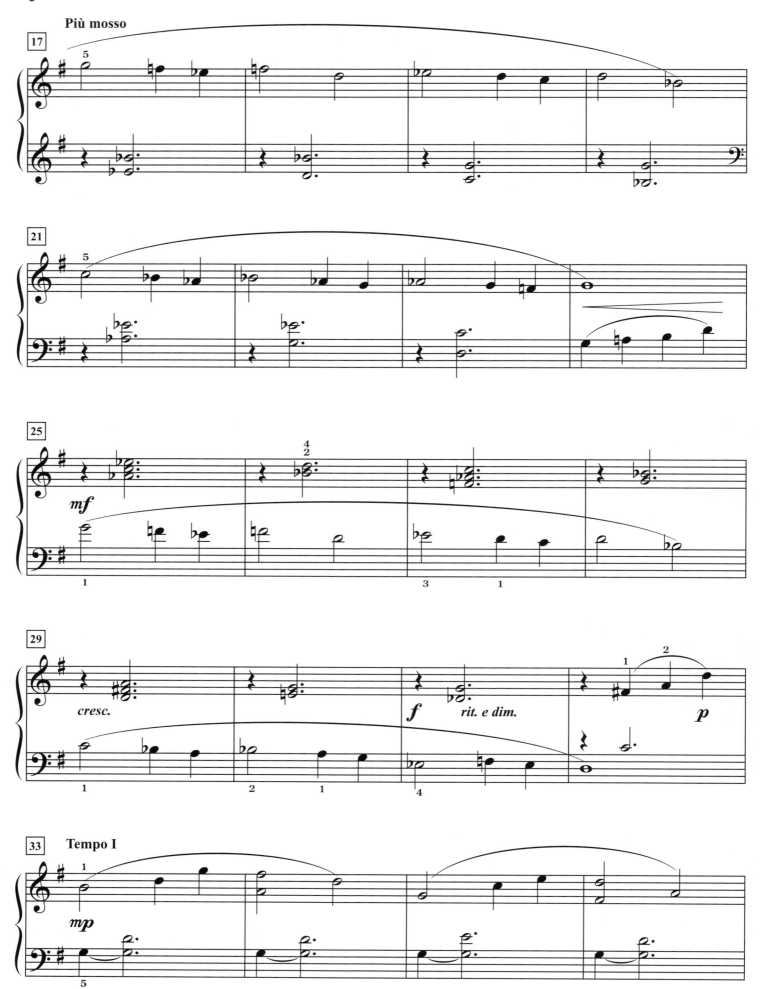

Light Air

Robert D. Vandall

9

Fond Memories

Robert D. Vandall

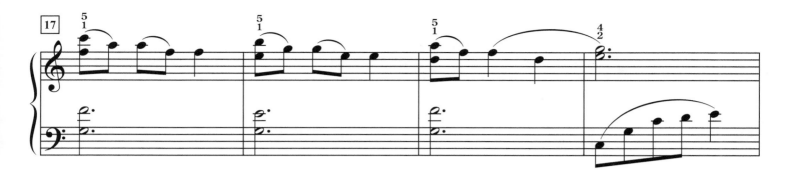

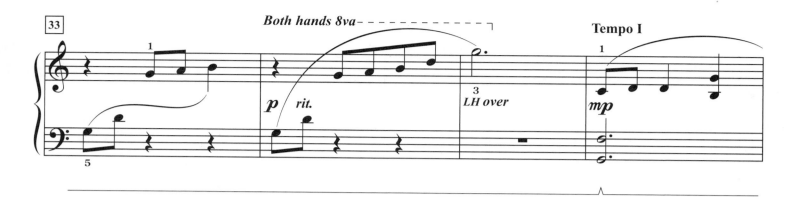

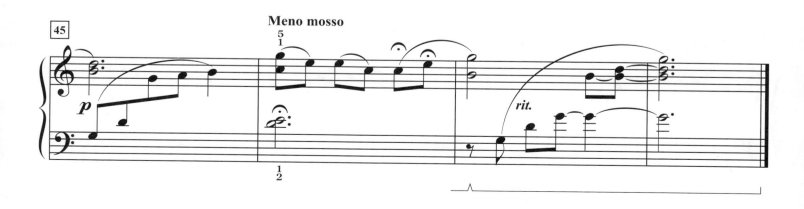

Dreamscape

Robert D. Vandall

Columbine Waltz

Robert D. Vandall

Waves in Sunlight

Robert D. Vandall

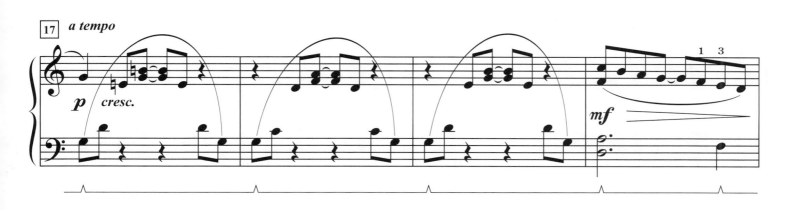

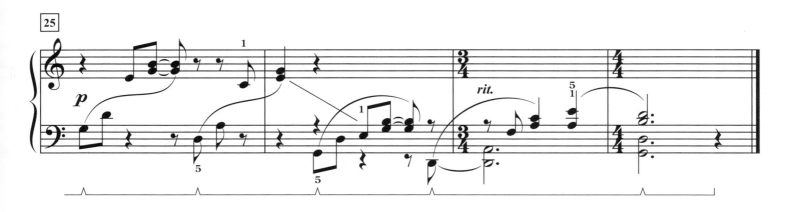

Red Rose Tango

Robert D. Vandall

Quiet Moments

Robert D. Vandall

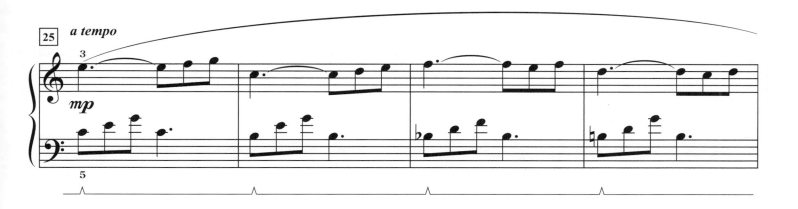